The West-Rising Sun

Darlene Cuevas

BookLeaf Publishing

Presentation by *BookLeaf Publishing*

Web: www.bookleafpub.com

E-mail: info@bookleafpub.com

ISBN: 9789357697330

First edition 2023

New Moon

Night falls
And maybe some of the stars too
It is another set of darkened hours
I am left wondering
If I will ever again see light

I tell this to you
Open up about how
Ever since I have learned
The art of worrying
That I never slept the same again

I feared sleep

Maybe it was because
Of how peaceful the silence was
Too peaceful for my liking

Or maybe it is the angst
And longing
For morning already

But this time
There is no peace
And even the mornings
Do not bring any relief

Cinder Cities

Night turns into day
Oh, so briefly

It is another dead star

Mother cannot even look through the window
She greets its fallen ashes
With weeping
Until she cannot breathe anymore

Father stares at it numbly
Straight into the blinding torture of loss
His irises taking over
And little girl cannot read him anymore

Little brother coos
Untroubled by mother's despair
Untroubled by father's resolution
Tethered by little sister's caress

Little girl wonders
If things truly must be this way

The city smells of burning concrete
Black embers and strangled schemes

The green, a mere daydream
Captured in sand through paintings

Little girl writes
She lets hope take over
As mother and father's retellings
Tell their own stories

A past
Where stars held hands
With the heavens
A future
Where earth is dancing
With the stars
And a recent tomorrow
That now unfurls
As every night turns into day

The Dream

I held my breath
As long as I could
And I now climb mountains in search
For the reason why
For the reason I like tasting
The saccharine darkness
In the orifices of twilight

I stayed up
As long as I could
And I now dig a hole in my mattress
Afraid of the world
Afraid of me
Trapped in the blood that drips
From these glass walls of winter

Growing up felt like the dream
The ultimate goal

Why did no one
Tell me otherwise
Save me from the disappointments
I now plant like landmines

Growing up was the dream

But right now
I just pray I wake up

February

Relegated to just numbers I can scroll through
These days eat themselves up like sand
Hollow and fluid and everything in between
I wonder if it really is supposed to be like this

My Box Full of Crayons

I wake up every day
With a box full of crayons
The dark room takes one
The empty table takes one
The hiding sun takes one
The stained mirror takes two

I hold this box full of crayons
Firmly with one hand
But life manages
To always find a way
So, it snatches some more
When I am not looking

Throughout the day
I try to stop myself
From sulking
As the vagabond takes one
As I give three to the child
As another car window takes two

These countless hours of classes
They take everything
Always leaving me with just one
And I make my way home

Wishing I can stitch this last piece
Beside my heart

I walk outside
And the fallen leaves
Give me back three
As the waning sun
Gives me two more

But when I enter home once again
The dark room takes one
The empty table takes one
The hiding sun takes one
The stained mirror takes two

And I always get left
Colouring my nights
Only with red

My Demons, They Sing

I'm too complex for you
And right from the start
Both of us knew that
I'm four steps ahead
Always, always steps ahead
While you trail behind

My mind races
And you hold my hand along
Hold me while I run
Patient as I eat pavement
And at the finish line
You're there
Cheering me on

I'm too complex for you
And we both knew
But still, we carried on
So, one knee
Down I went
You leaped and kneeled down too

We wrote forever
In an infinity loop
I do, say I do

Yes, I do

And years later we grow
Two multiplied by one and a half
If you add the pet
Make that multiplied by two

Our child grows
And we tag along
The way the moon follows the sun
The mornings overflow with laughter
Lunchtime is quiet
The evenings are quieter
But we drink it because that's all we have known

My complexity's a curse
And you brave the witch
But it stays because maybe I embrace it too
My complexity's a curse
And you brave the wizard
But it stays because maybe I like myself like this
too

I love you
Have I told you that today
I know I have had
But still

I love you

I lie in bed beside your form
The quintessence of calm and life and joy
Why did you stay
I wonder at nights like this
When my head and soul wander daunting paths

I'm too complex for you
And we both knew
So, I wake you up and ask you to stay
And hold me close
In your safe embrace
Like wind favouring one tree

What do I bring you
I ask
Not the first time

You bring me breadth
More than the universe can
When I hold you, you feel like molten starlight
You flow and surround me
Carve me in place
I dive the canyon of queries
And I see such dimension and light

So, my love, never dare me

And ask why I stay
Because you're too complex for me
And we both knew

But I'm only brave enough
To thread turbid shallows
And we both knew that as well

Midnight Vodka

I look at you
And I wonder
How hard it was
How hard life was
Because you never talk about it

How much hope and positivity
Do I have to drink
To get to that point
Where all of right now is enough
To drown all of yesterday's pain

Fallback

When the fighter gets tired of fighting
And the saviour starts to need saving
Who will be there

The Fire That Devours

Dancing in the fire
That burns for our love
I revel in the pain
And in the valour

I remember years past
Of headaches from worry
Sadness stretching, feeding
On my tired mind

I colour, I cry
Fabricate inspiring lies
Wanting you
Yet not looking for me

I sleep a restless sleep
Vomit feelings on my sheets
A clawing, a misery
I leave stomachs deep

I tried for words
Stick figures and hymns
Hide my rainbows
When skyscrapers roam

To seek, to not want
To forsake, to not love
I eat every city
To feel my heart

I hold you in my dreams
In pink clouds, in the fog
You sing to me
Dance, run, jump, scream

The Fire That Makes

I remember these years past
Of headaches from melancholy
Fatigue stretching, feeding
On my tired life

I now dance in the fire
That burns for our love
I revel in the intensity
And in the spasmodic respite

I paint, I try
Living what once were lies
Wanting you
Yet wanting myself more

I dream in nights like this
Warmth within our sheets
A gnawing, an overflow
I leave bare

I walk with words
Stick figures and hymns
Let our rainbows decide
When skyscrapers roam

To have and to want
To not forsake and to love
I let every city
Take parts of my heart

I now hold you close
In pink button ups under stars
You sing to me
It's okay to need someone

November Blue

I read somewhere
That saying life is unfair
Is childish
Is whiny
Is weak

I held this for so long
I detested the word
Unfair
Because it is childish
It is whiny
It is weak
Right

But I write this down
On the notes app
Of my scarlet red smartphone
At the farthest seat
On the first bus I take
From school going home

And I think about how
I could be in bed by now
If only I had my own car
I would not then

Have had to endure
This bus ride that suffocates me
With the overwhelm of real life
Every single time

I write this down on my phone
Enveloped in four layers of clothing
And I cannot help
But think about life
And that it is indeed unfair
As I pass every lost person
In just one layer of clothing
Who will be walking eternally

Motion sickness holds my hands now
But it will pass
And I cannot help
But think about life
And that it is indeed unfair
Because some pains out there
Will never pass
Meant to be felt eternally

There's a snowstorm outside
And its anger is beautiful
White, silver, grey, black

And I hate that we still love life
After everything vile it has fed us

The same way we still love winter
Even with the shadows
Of November blue

Fixed by a Triangle Stone

They don't understand us
And they never might be
So, I dream of buying
An expanse of land by the sea

Something by a waterfall
Would also make do
At the ends of our world
I'll build a house with bamboo

I would wake up in the mornings
And make chai tea
Unworried if my choice of song
Touches all my trinkets sharply

I would welcome indigo evenings
And dance between doors
Not worried if my feet
Are too loud on golden floors

I would enjoy the silence
Whenever I decide to
And enjoy all of its counterparts
Just the same

A tiny house
At the ends of our world
I know in my heart
Is enough to hold me sane

Lesser Than

In a sea of faces
Under veils of presumptions
You, yourself, create

It is harrowing to think
And to realize
That someone out there
Has more than you

Grateful is the peace you feel
In a crowded room of glitter
Grateful is the peace you feel
In a crowded room devoid of colour

It is harrowing even more to think
And to realize
That someone out there
Has less than you

Yet here you are
Drowning in a sea of faces
Under veils of presumptions
You, yourself, create

Earth-Bound

Every night of this existence
I lay my heavy soul to sleep
I burry all of my defeats
And plant daffodils
Hoping their roots run deep

Deep enough to taste my pain
Hold it in a tired embrace

We all are trying
I know that by now
It's just heartbreaking how
The measures of better and greater
Maybe do not exist at all

Words never fail me
Only the world can

So, I dig another hole
For my next battle

I pick at my imperfect, painted nails
Bloody red, sorrowful red
Now with the gloom
And darkness of soil

What a perfect sight
It is indeed
These clawing shards
In the graveyard of my dreams

I'd Know My Way Around

I'd know my way around
With eyes closed
Heart open
Know every chipped part of the walls
Every little gap between the wooden floors

I tried it out tonight
I even knew how many steps
It would take
To get to the fridge
For me to leave

One hand covering my face
I traced everything
Knew perfectly how high each light switch was
Knew the scent of each room
And the soft changes in the air

We built me up
For so long
You taught me to love myself
By loving me
But I hate this

I hate the way I know it all

The way I know my way around
Your home
Which was once
Ours

This Is the Pain, Speaking

I don't recognize it anymore
The eyes staring back at me
I search for any ounce of familiarity
Alas, nothing

I put my hair up
And colour my eyelids blue
Powdering my nose
Lips tinted a rosy hue

My heart, it skips beats
Here and there
And I feel like I'm drowning
Although I'm in air

I pick up my keys
Check all the stoves, wires, and heat
Bid my plants a little farewell
I'll be back soon

I drive to the grocery
With windows down
Swallowing the bitter air
I deserve this

I walk towards the automatic doors
Smile at the shrub there
My feet taking me naturally
Along arrows our dreams already know

I pick up peonies
And some lilacs
Grab a cheesecake too
By the baker's aisle

And I drive to your place
To say I'm sorry
For the awful things I said
The other night

I do regret them, but I did mean them
And I'm wishing now that you forget
The way you have forgotten my pain
Every single time

So, I kneel at the door
Ready to take you back
And I ring the bell
As you await

Then I said
Hello
It was the pain speaking
Speaking the truth

The Cliffs We Climb at Midnight

Let's fall in love
With life again

I dare myself
As I stare at the ceiling
The ceiling of my empty, heated room
Illuminated by a waning moon
Under layers of sheets, I sink
But why do I feel cold?

I resist the urge to grab my phone
Yet, the lovesick demon wins again
She thirsts for more
For so much more
But she does not know for what exactly
So, she whispers to me
Let's check our socials
We promise that light and joy are there

I live through other people's lives
Vicariously
As I scroll and scroll and scroll

The family clock ticks away outside

Filling the home's walls, tocks
They have become monotone now

The hours dwindle away
Along with my sanity
The aforesaid challenge no longer standing

The sun now speaks to the moon
Go to sleep
But it's I who need it more

My eyes are sore
My head, pounding
But my wrist can keep going
My fingers keep scrolling
And my thirst feels evermore

The sunrise now shouts at my ceiling
What are you doing, let go
The glare, too unfathomable

I scream at the demon
Threatened her like I did yesterday's dawn,
The dawn of the day before yesterday,
And the day before that too

Let's fall in love
With life again

A lullaby I sing myself to sleep
The words floundering about
In the ocean of my tears
The world crumbling around
In my fatigued everything

Please, please
Let's fall in love with life again

So, I wake hours later
When the sun is at its peak
I envy her, for she never gets tired

I spring to my feet
Do eight jumping jacks
I got this, I got this
As I scream a silent scream

I look at the clock
12:38
Earlier than yesterday, the day before yesterday,
And the day before that too

I brush my teeth, wash my face clean
With the coldest the water can go
I fix my bed, tuck away another night of defeats
Spray my favourite lavender scent
Hoping the droplets chase them away

The wintry scene through the windows speaks to
me
And at this time of day
I am friends with the demon
She praises me for another battle won
And cries because she knows
I will always win
This diurnal battle, this deep never-ending leap

She screams through her tears

Let's fall in love
With life again

The West-Rising Sun

The mountains of what I have achieved
I float before them
And instead of rejoicing
I strive only to make more mountains rise

Graveyards devour the demesnes below
Where lay starving dreams, empty breaths
All my pain and defeats bow before me
I count to a perpetual curse

Flowers litter
One, two, three, four
Five, six, seven, eight, nine
An ennead for each and every tear

The twilight says it is nigh
The night promises the dawn
To look back, step down, hold onto severed
hopes
Only the sun knows how to make my soul sing